"It's foolish to go out on the water without a life jacket; it is even more foolish to try to sail the sea of life without Jesus."
- Anonymous

The Bible Alphabet Coloring Book

To order additional books:
www.amazon.com
www.theanchorgathering.com

To find out more about The Anchor Gathering or Katie's book and Bible studies,
visit www.theanchorgathering.com

Other books by Katie Robertson:
Anchored: Walking by Faith, Living in Hope, Remembering Karina
Live Anchored: A Bible Study
Jesus, Our Anchor.

ISBN: 9781952943058

Book Packaging: Inspira Literary Solutions, Gig Harbor, WA
Printed in the USA by Ingram Spark

Psalm 78:4

We will not hide these truths from our children;
We will tell the next generation about the glorious deeds of the Lord,
about His power and His mighty wonders.

Deuteronomy 4:9

Be careful, and watch yourselves closely so that you do not forget
the things your eyes have seen or let them slip from your heart
as long as you live. Teach them to your children
and to their children after them."

Dedicated to my children:
Karina, Annika, and Erik.

And to my grandchildren;
may you always remain anchored in Jesus.

Love the Lord your God with all your heart and with all your soul and with all your strength. These commandments that I give you today are to be upon your hearts. Impress them on your children. Talk about them when you sit at home and when you walk along the road, when you lie down and when you get up.

Deuteronomy 6:5-7

A is for Angel

An ANGEL of the Lord appeared to the shepherds saying: Do not be afraid, I bring good news of great joy. Today in the city of David, the Christ child is born unto you.

Luke 2:9,10

B is for Believe

For God so loved the world that he gave His only son, that whoever BELIEVES in Him will never die but have eternal life.

John 3:16

C is for Children

Let the little CHILDREN come to me, and do not hinder them, for the kingdom of heaven belongs to such as these.

Matthew 19:14

D is for Disciple

By this all men will know that you are my DISCIPLES,
if you love one another.

John 13:3

E is for Everlasting

I tell you the truth; He who believes has EVERLASTING life.

John 6:47

F is for FAITH

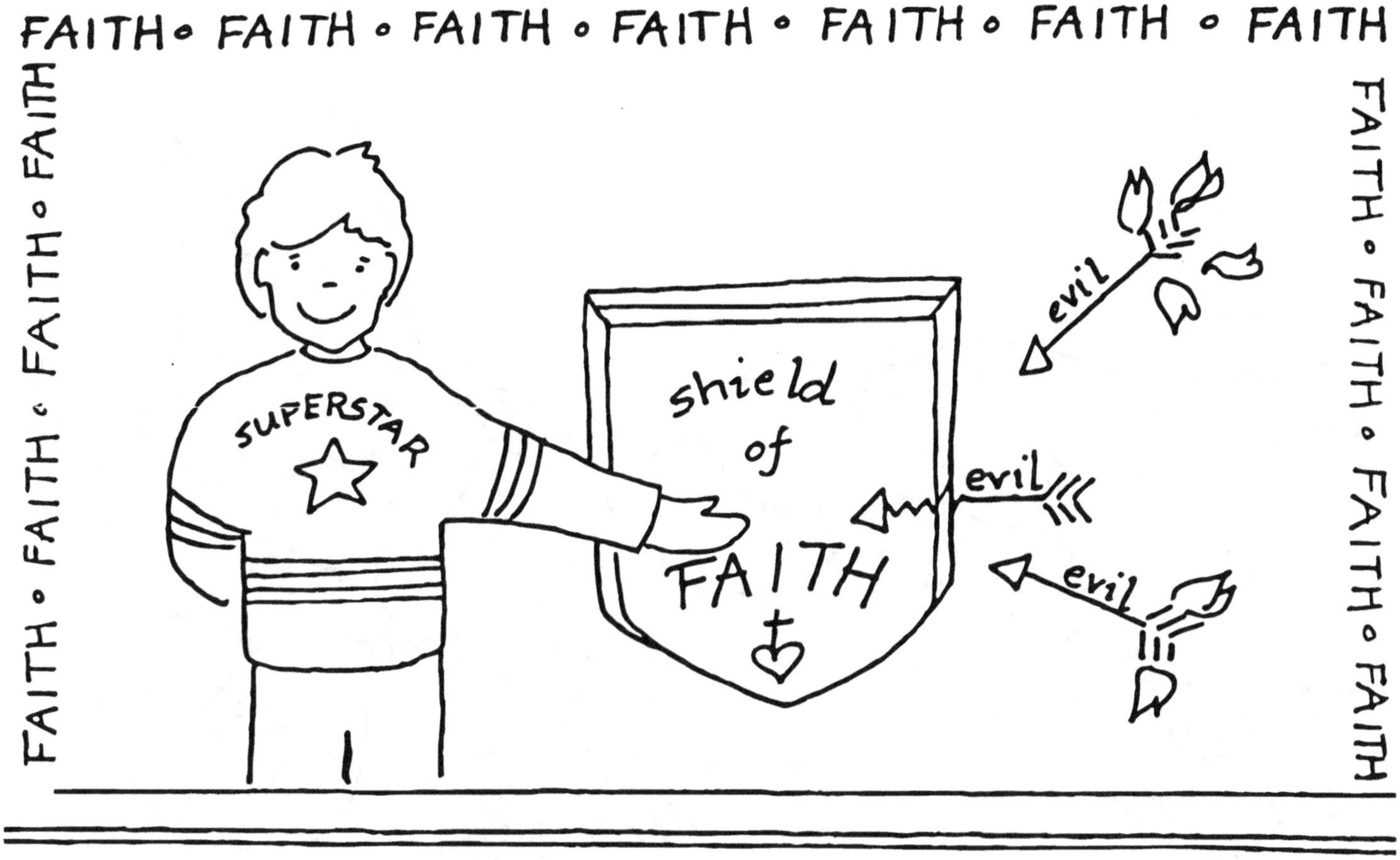

Take up your shield of FAITH with which you can extinguish all the flaming arrows of the evil one.

Ephesians 6:16

G is for Goodness

The fruits of the spirit are: love, joy, peace, patience, kindness, GOODNESS, faithfulness, gentleness, and self-control.

Galatians 5:22

H is for Heart

Heart ∘ ♡ ∘ Heart ∘ ♡ ∘ Heart ∘ ♡ ∘ Heart ∘ ♡ ∘

Love the Lord your God with all your HEART, soul, mind, strength, and love your neighbor as yourself.

Matthew 22:37

I is for Immanuel

IMMANUEL JESUS IMMANUEL JESUS

The virgin Mary will be with child and will give birth to a son, and they will call Him IMMANUEL—which means God with us.

Matthew 1:23

J is for JOY

Shout for JOY to God all the earth! Sing the glory of His name, make His praise glorious!

Psalm 66:1-2

K is for KING

God is the blessed, and only ruler, the KING of kings and Lord of lords, who alone is immortal and who lives in unapproachable light, whom no one has seen or can see. To Him be honor and might!

1 Timothy 6:16

L is for Light

And Jesus said, " I am the LIGHT of the world whoever follows me will never walk in darkness but will have the light of life."

John 8:12

M is for Mighty

Finally, be strong in the Lord and in his MIGHTY power. Put on the full armor of God so that you can take your stand against the devil.

Ephesians 6:10

N is for New

Therefore, if anyone is in Christ, he is a NEW creation, the old has gone the new has come.

2 Corinthians 5:17

O is for Obey

Children OBEY your parents in the Lord, for this is right. Honor your father and mother—which is the first commandment with a promise—that it may go well with you to enjoy long life.

Ephesians 6:1-3

P is for Pray

Be joyful always; PRAY continually; give thanks in all circumstances, for this is God's will for you in Christ Jesus.

1 Thessalonians 5:16-17

Q is for Qualities

Make every effort to add to your faith goodness, and knowledge, self-control, perseverance, godliness, brotherly kindness, and love. For if you possess these QUALITIES in increasing measure, they will keep you from being ineffective and unproductive in your knowledge of the Lord Jesus.

2 Peter 1:5-8

R is for Rejoice

Allelujah!

REJOICE ♪ REJOICE ♫ REJOICE ♫♪

REJOICE in the Lord always; I will say it again

REJOICE!!

Philippians 4:4

S is for Seek

SEEK first His kingdom and His righteousness,
andall these things will be given to you as well.

Matthew 6:33

T is for Trust

We trust our heart to you, Lord!

TRUST in the Lord with all your heart and lean not on your own understanding. Acknowledge the Lord in all of your ways and he will make your path straight.

Proverbs 3:5-6

U is for Unity

May the God who gives endurance and encouragement give you a spirit of UNITY among yourselves as you follow Christ Jesus.

Romans 15:5

V is for Victory

Thanks be to God! He is gives us VICTORY through our Lord Jesus Christ. Therefore my dear brothers, stand firm. Let nothing move you. Always give yourself fully to the work of the Lord.

1 Corinthians 15:57-58

W is for Worship

Come let us bow down in WORSHIP; let us kneel before the Lord our Maker, for He is our God and we are the people of His pasture and flock under his care.

Psalm 95:6

X is for eXalt

Glorify the Lord with me; and let us EXALT His name together!

Psalm 34:3

Y is for Young

Don't let anyone look down on you because you are YOUNG, but set an example for the believers, in life, in love, in faith, and purity.

1 Timothy 4:12

Z is for Zeal

Never be lacking in ZEAL, but keep your spiritual excitement, serving the Lord.

Romans 12:11

TIPS FOR ANCHORING

1. It's never too early to start talking to kids about the Lord, helping them to know how loved they are, and what a special plan God has for their lives.
   (Jeremiah 29:11)

2. Help them memorize Scripture. From age two and up, kids can easily repeat short phrases and songs. This Scripture, once hidden in their hearts, will stay with them their whole lives.
   (Psalm 119:11)

3. Teach your kids the simplicity of prayer, that they can comes to the Lord with all of their cares and concerns and also with thankfulness for the many blessings of life.
   (1Peter 5:7)

4. Teach kids to combat fear with what is true... you can nip anxiety in the bud by teaching them to hold firmly to truth.
   (Philippians 4:8)

5. Teach them the importance of time with the Lord. Kids love the idea of finding their own special, secret place where they can meet for quiet time with the Lord. Give your kids a children's Bible and a journal and teach them to write their thoughts and prayers in it. Help them cultivate a personal relationship with the Lord. As they get older, this can be a habit that keeps them anchored.
   (Matthew 6:6)

6. Focus on the faithfulness of God in your own life and share stories about answered prayers, "God moments," and stories from the Bible or things you read about others' experiences of His faithfulness.
   (Lamentations 21-23)

YOUR CHILDREN IN FAITH

7. Make the most of every opportunity to show kids how God is in the details of life, and impress upon them how deeply He desires to be in relationship with us. Don't be shy about helping kids invite Christ into their heart.
(Deuteronomy 6:6-9)

8. Take the time for daily devotional readings together, talking about the Lord openly and showing how He is real.
(Proverbs 22:6)

9. Point out the wonders of creation and the amazing patterns and things in nature that point to designs of a Master Builder and Creator.
(Psalm 19:1-2)

10. Make learning about God fun with songs, plays, puppet shows, and movies.
(Colossians 3:23)

11. Be intentional about giving kids a wide exposure to faith activities through involvement like church, summer camps, special speakers, and concerts.
(Hebrews 10:23-24)

12. Treat your family like a team: get your kids to support each other like they would teammates. Eat together. Make time for shared activities, vacations, play, and conversation.
(Ephesians 4:2-3)

About the Author

Katie Robertson created this Bible Alphabet Coloring Book for her oldest daughter, Karina, when she was two years old, to help anchor her in the truths of Jesus. Her hope and prayer is that you, too, will enjoy this book and use it to teach and encourage your children and their children, to anchor their faith in Jesus and the truths that hold us strong in this stormy world.

Katie is a former teacher who has devoted the current season of her life to speaking, mentoring, and serving in her community, bringing hope and inspiration for living a life anchored by faith in Jesus Christ. She is the author of *Anchored: Walking by Faith, Living in Hope, Remembering Karina,* a book about the life of Katie's daughter Karina, who went to be with Jesus in 2010. Katie is also the author of two Bible studies: *Live Anchored: A Bible Study,* and *Jesus, Our Anchor.*

Katie founded and directs The Anchor (www.theanchorgathering.com), a gathering for women of all ages and backgrounds to encourage and anchor them in faith and friendship. The Anchor has multiple locations in the Pacific Northwest (and growing!). A graduate of the University of Washington, Katie is also a runner, artist, the mother of two grown children, and the delighted grandmother of two precious little girls.

Katie and her husband, Ron, live in Gig Harbor, Washington, where they continue to enjoy their seaside home and boating adventures. You can contact her through her website, https://www.theanchorgathering.com.

www.ingramcontent.com/pod-product-compliance
Lightning Source LLC
Chambersburg PA
CBHW081759100526
44592CB00015B/2495
* 9 7 8 1 9 5 2 9 4 3 0 5 8 *